Staffing Skills IT Managers Must Have

Tips And Techniques That IT Managers Can Use In Order To Correctly Staff Their Teams

"Practical, proven techniques that will help you to attract and retain the right staff"

Dr. Jim Anderson

Published by:
Blue Elephant Consulting
Tampa, Florida

Copyright © 2013 by Dr. Jim Anderson

All rights reserved. No part of this book may be reproduced of transmitted in any form or by any means, electronic or mechanical, including photocopying, recording or by any information storage and retrieval system without written permission of the publisher, except for inclusion of brief quotations in a review.

Printed in the United States of America

Library of Congress Control Number: 2013957208

ISBN-13: 978-1494424268

ISBN-10: 1494424266

Warning – Disclaimer

The purpose of this book is to educate and entertain. This book does not promise or guarantee that anyone following the ideas, tips, suggestions, techniques or strategies will be successful. The author, publisher and distributor(s) shall have neither liability nor responsibility to anyone with respect to any loss or damage caused, or alleged to be caused, directly or indirectly by the information contained in this book.

Recent Books By The Author

Product Management

- Product Development Lessons For Product Managers: How Product Managers Can Create Successful Products

- Customer Lessons For Product Managers: Techniques For Product Managers To Better Understand What Their Customers Really Want

Public Speaking

- How To Give A Great Presentation: Presentation techniques that will transform a speech into a memorable event

- How To Rehearse In Order To Give The Perfect Speech: How to effectively rehearse your next speech to that your message be remembered forever!

CIO Skills

- Critical CIO Management Skills: Decision Making Skills That Every CIO Needs To Have In Order To Be Able To Make The Right Choices

- How CIOs Can Make Innovation Happen: Tips And Techniques For CIOs To Use In Order To Make Innovation Happen In Their

T Department

IT Manager Skills

- Secrets Of Effective Leadership For IT Managers: Tips And Techniques That IT Managers Can Use In Order To Develop Leadership Skills

- IT Manager Career Secrets: Tips And Techniques That IT Managers Can Use In Order To Have A Successful Career

Negotiating

- Learn How To Argue In Your Next Negotiation: How To Develop The Skill Of Effective Arguing In A Negotiation In Order To Get The Best Possible Outcome

- How To Open Your Next Negotiation: How To Start A Negotiation In Order To Get The Best Possible Outcome

Miscellaneous

- Power Distribution Unit (PDU) Secrets: What Everyone Who Works In A Data Center Needs To Know!

- Making The Jump: How To Land Your Dream Job When You Get Out Of College!

Note: See a complete list of books by Dr. Jim Anderson at the back of this book.

Acknowledgements

Any book like this one is the result of years of real-world work experience. In my over 25 years of working for 7 different firms, I have met countless fantastic people and I've been mentored by some truly exceptional ones. Although I've probably forgotten some of the people who made me the person that I am today, here is my attempt to finally give them the recognition that they so truly deserve:

- Thomas P. Anderson
- Art Puett
- Bobbi Marshall
- Bob Boggs

Dr. Jim Anderson

This book is dedicated to my wife Lori. None of this would have been possible without her love and support.

Thanks for the best 21 years of my life (so far)...!

Table Of Contents

AN IT MANAGER IS ONLY AS GOOD AS HIS / HER TEAM 8

ABOUT THE AUTHOR 10

CHAPTER 1: HE'S / SHE'S LEAVING? NOW WHAT? 15

CHAPTER 2: RETENTION, RETENTION, RETENTION 17

CHAPTER 3: Q: WHAT'S WORSE THAN AN UNHAPPY WORKER LEAVING? A: IF THEY STAY... 20

CHAPTER 4: "YOU'RE FIRED!" (HOW TO LET PEOPLE GO WITH CLASS) 23

CHAPTER 5: MANAGING IT TALENT IN THE 21ST CENTURY: GROW OR BUY? 26

CHAPTER 6: STAFFING FLEXIBILITY IS SOOOO UNDERRATED!...........30

CHAPTER 7: WHAT SHOULD AN IT MANAGER LOOK FOR WHEN HIRING EMPLOYEES? 34

CHAPTER 8: 5 CHARACTERISTICS OF HARD CORE GAMERS THAT IT MANAGERS NEED..38

CHAPTER 9: THE IT MANAGER'S DILEMMA: SMART PEOPLE OR GOOD IDEAS? 41

CHAPTER 10: ARE IT MANAGERS AFRAID OF COMMITMENT? EMPLOYEES SPEAK UP 45

CHAPTER 11: WHY ARE THERE SO FEW WOMEN IN IT? 48

CHAPTER 12: GOOGLE'S STAFFING PROBLEMS CAN TEACH IT LEADERS A LOT..52

An IT Manager Is Only As Good As His / Her Team

All too often we find ourselves in the position of being an IT manager with little or no training on what it takes to correctly staff a team. This is a critical skill for us to have. Ultimately, the success of an IT manager rests on how his / her team preforms.

You might think that staffing is all about hiring the right people to come and join your team. It turns out that there is a lot more to this. Staffing involves attracting and retaining the right people. However, it also deals with knowing when it is time to let the wrong members of your team go.

Knowing what to look for when it comes time to staff your team is a critical IT manager skill. You need to understand how important flexibility is because, as with all such things in life, everything continues to change over time. The best IT team members can come from unusual places and you need to know where to look for them.

IT managers have to deal with the classic dilemma: should you be looking for the smartest people or the people who have the best ideas? They are not necessarily the same group of people. While you are at it, will you be doing anything to solve the problem of there being too few women in IT?

We can all take heart in the fact that we are not alone in facing the challenges of creating a highly effective IT team. Even at companies as big and successful as Google they are struggling with this challenge and we can learn a lot from how they are tacking it.

This book has been written to provide you with the skills that you are going to need in order to be able to attract, hire, retain, and motive a group of workers who will ultimately make your manager career a success. We'll investigate what you need to be looking for in new staff members and how you can get the most out of the team members that you already have.

For more information on what it takes to be a great IT manager, check out my blog, The Accidental IT Leader, at:

www.TheAccidentalITLeader.com

Good luck!

- Dr. Jim Anderson

About The Author

I must confess that I never set out to be a CIO. When I went to school, I studied Computer Science and thought that I'd get a nice job programming and that would be that. Well, at least part of that plan worked out!

My first job was working for Boeing on their F/A-18 fighter jet program. I spent my days programming fighter jet software in assembly language and I loved it. The U.S. government decided to save some money and went looking for other countries to sell this plane to. This put me into an unfamiliar role: I started to meet with foreign military officials and I ended up having to manage groups of engineers who were working on international projects.

Time moved on and so did I. I found myself working for Siemens, the big German telecommunications company. They were making phone switches and selling them to the seven U.S. phone companies. The problem was that the switches were too complicated. Customers couldn't tell the difference between one complicated phone switch from another complicated phone switch. Once again I found myself working with the sales and marketing teams to find ways to make the great technology that the engineers had developed understandable to both internal and external customers.

I've spent over 25 years working as an senior IT professional for both big companies and startups. This has given me an opportunity to learn what it takes to manage and IT department in ways that allow it to maximize its output while becoming a valuable part of the overall company.

I now live in Tampa Florida where I spend my time managing my consulting business, Blue Elephant Consulting, teaching college courses at the University of South Florida, and traveling to work with companies like yours to share the knowledge that I have about how to create and manage successful IT departments.

I'm always available to answer questions and I can be reached at:

Dr. Jim Anderson
Blue Elephant Consulting
Email: jim@BlueElephantConsulting.com
Facebook: http://goo.gl/1TVoK
Web: **www.BlueElephantConsulting.com**

"Unforgettable communication skills that will set your ideas free…"

Create IT Departments That Are Productive And A Valuable Asset To The Rest Of The Company !

Dr. Jim Anderson is available to provide training and coaching on the topics that are the most important to people who have to manage IT departments: how can I build a productive IT department (and keep it together) while at the same time providing the rest of the company with the IT services that they need?

Dr. Anderson believes that in order to both learn and remember what he says, speakers need to laugh. Each one of his speeches is full of fun and humor so that what he says "sticks" with everyone.

Dr. Anderson's CIO SkillsTraining Includes:

1. How to identify and attract the right type of IT workers to your IT department.
2. How to build relationships with the company's senior management in order to get the support that you need?
3. How to stay on top of changing technology and security issues so that you never get surprised?

Dr. Jim Anderson works with over 100 customers per year. To invite Dr. Anderson to work with you, contact him at:

Phone: 813-418-6970 or
Email: jim@BlueElephantConsulting.com

Blue Elephant Consulting
Speaking. Negotiating. Managing. Marketing.

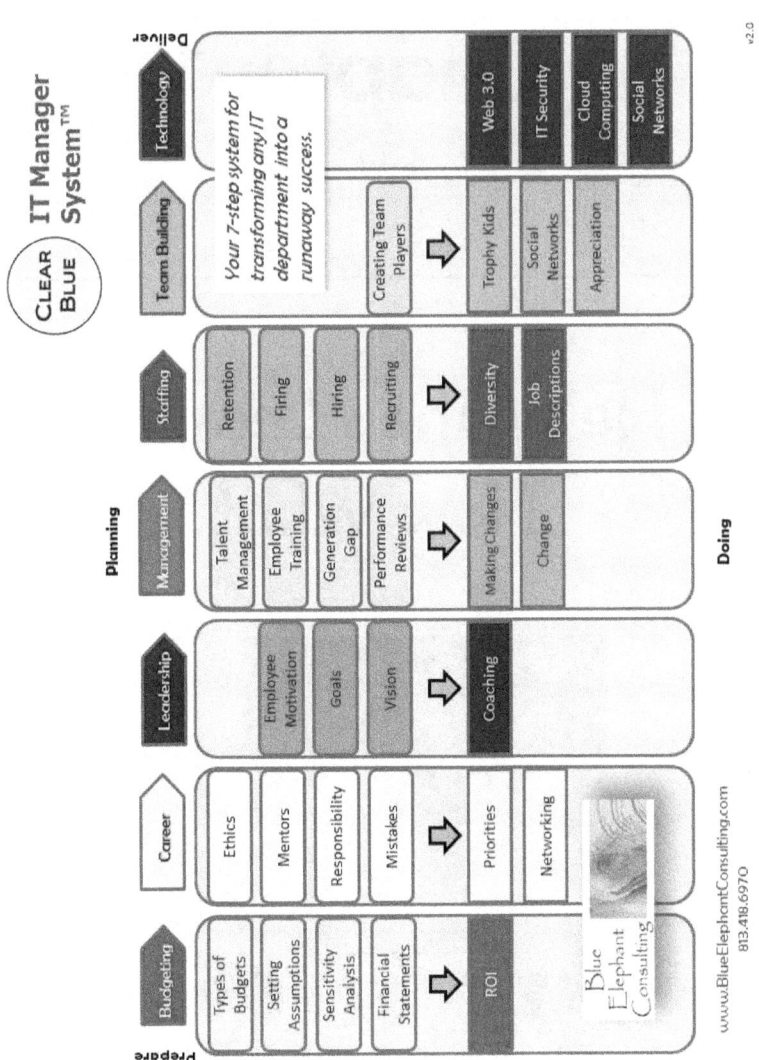

The **Clear Blue IT Manager System™** has been created to provide IT managers with a clear roadmap for how to manage an IT team. This system shows IT Managers what needs to be done and in what order to do it.

Chapter 1

He's / She's Leaving? Now What?

Chapter 1: He's / She's Leaving? Now What?

Teams are a wonderful thing — when everyone is linked together and plays off of each other's strengths an IT department can virtually hum just like a smooth flowing machine. However, when a team member decides to leave the team, whether it's to go to another internal team or to go to a new company, it can cause the whole department engine to start to sputter and misfire.

For those who are left on the team, the loss of a team member who has chosen to leave the team can be difficult to deal with. A good IT manager has to recognize that envy will immediately show up: we all are jealous of others who appear to be heading for greener pastures / better challenges / more money.

The most effective way to deal with this is to let it happen, wait for the person to actually physically leave, and then reveal / discuss new exciting challenges for the remaining team. Envy is a short term emotion and can be quickly buried if you can get the team excited about another project task.

The next big question is how does the loss of the team member impact the team? Specifically, who will be picking up the work that the leaving team member was working on?

Additionally, does this loss of a team member open the door for any promotions? Answers to both of these issues need to be determined as quickly as possible and communicated to the whole team early on.

There is a lot more to do, but these are two good places to start.

Chapter 2

Retention, Retention, Retention

Chapter 2: Retention, Retention, Retention

So you've finally built a great IT team and now you can't sleep at night because you are worried that everyone is going to leave. Well guess what, you're probably right — everyone will eventually leave; however, how fast they leave depends on you.

The IT field has a rich history of job hopping and even in today's lean times, this has not changed. Unfortunately it's your most valuable employees that will be most likely to hop because they have the talents & experience that your competition is looking for. What's an IT manager to do?

IT workers are a unique breed. If they like what they are doing, they will stay.

One of the first ways to ensure that this happens is to make sure that everyone's connected with the mission of the business. Note that this is easy to say, but can be very hard to do.

The larger the firm, the more disconnected most workers feel. Please keep in mind that the mission of the business can never have anything to do with money (i.e. "Grow profits by 20%") because unless you work in accounting, you can never get excited about that.

Next is to make sure that IT management is open with the staff about business wins, losses, and hiring plans. When was the last time that you sat down with your staff and talked about where the company is going?

For that matter, do you even know where the company is headed? If everyone feels as though they know what is going on, then they will better understand how their job is helping the company get there.

Once again, please note that saying that you have an "open door" policy is really just so many words. Your actions will speak much louder than these words.

Promoting from within can be a key tool for getting folks to stick around. If everyone knows what a career path looks like at your company, then they will know where they stand and what their chances of moving up are. If you are constantly hiring from the outside to fill upper management positions, then the team will lose heart and move on.

Finally, be very careful when it comes to team building activities. IT staff are notorious for not wanting to participate in these events and if you are not careful, it could turn into something that looks like a scene from "The Office" TV Show .

Instead, creating a challenge that requires a team to work together in order to win a prize or reward that has visibility (big trophy displayed in the office) or has a clear social value (donation to a charity in their names) can make a lasting impression.

One of the things that makes an IT team so valuable is its creativity ("innovation" in modern speak). If you use this same creativity to actively work to create an environment in which the IT staff wants to keep working and looks forward to what comes next, then congratulations — you've succeeded.

Chapter 3

Q: What's Worse Than An Unhappy Worker Leaving?
A: If They Stay...

Chapter 3: Q: What's Worse Than An Unhappy Worker Leaving? A: If They Stay...

We all know that having high turnover can at best be disruptive and at worst can throw projects off schedule, kill budgets, and doom overall employee morale. So you would think that if you are somehow able to have a low number of employees leaving that everything would be hunky dory, right?

Wrong — you might now have lots of unhappy employees who have for one reason or another decided that they can't leave right now. They'll keep coming into work each day (or logging on if they are unhappily telecommuting), but they will be dragging their virtual feet and just going through the motions. They are not going to be helping the company be a success.

Why are so many non-leaving employees unhappy? I think that I know the reason and the author Patrick Lencioni has captured them quite nicely in his book "**The Three Signs of a Miserable Job**".

In his book, Patrick states that he believes that people become unhappy in their jobs when their basic social needs are not being met. Yeah, yeah, yeah — we all love a paycheck and the bigger the better. However, we really go to work in order to have some very basic human needs met: to get a sense of accomplishment, to boost self-esteem, and to feel that we are part of a community.

When we aren't getting these needs met, Patrick calls the problems "anonymity, irrelevance, and immeasurability". Great, now you've got the silent problem of unhappy IT workers lurking in your department. What to do?

Don't despair! In order to reach out and change unhappy workers into committed employees you have to tackle these key issues one by one.

One-on-one feedback is the key to providing employees with both a sense of accomplishment (they know who I am!) and boosting self-esteem (they like what I do!). Developing a sense of community is somewhat more difficult — in the IT field if this is done incorrectly; it can come across as fake.

However, if done correctly you can turn a lackluster department into a team of overachievers. Now that's something to cheer about!

Chapter 4

"You're Fired!" (How To Let People Go With Class)

Chapter 4: "You're Fired!" (How To Let People Go With Class)

Ouch! one of the worst parts about being an IT manager is when it comes time to fire someone. It really doesn't matter if the person truly deserves it or this is one of those "cut 10% from every department" exercises.

Handling the situation where staff decides to leave by themselves is hard enough, this just makes a manager's life that much more complicated. Some companies have training for their IT managers on how to handle this part of their job correctly; however, most just leave it up to the individual managers to learn how to do it over time.

If we can agree that there is no easy way to turn life upside down for somebody that you work with, then at least we can take a moment and talk about a few guidelines for how you can terminate people with some measure of class for both you and them.

- **Best Time To Fire Someone**: hands down its best done at the end of the day. Most often the person is going to be in shock and will need time alone to deal with what has just happened to them. Going home is better than sitting around at work. Additionally, if they need to clean out their desk, then they don't have to put up with EVERYONE dropping by to tell them how sorry they are for them / glad that it wasn't them.

- **Have A Good Reason For The Firing**: Being fired is hard enough for IT professionals, but not being given a reason for your termination seems to make it 10x worse. A weak excuse like "I was told to fire you" or something like that is no better having no good reason.

- **Do The Firing Face-To-Face**: The IT industry is full of really bad ways to fire people using technology. Bad examples include leaving voicemails telling people that they've been let go and sending termination notices out via email. As much as it hurts to deliver this news in person, it is really the right way to do it.

One of the best ways of thinking about why it's important to do a good job of firing people was said by Bob Wilson who is the Chief Human Resources Officer for Elliott Davis: "We never want to lose sight of the fact that the person is forever an alumni." Amen to that brother.

Chapter 5

Managing IT Talent In The 21st Century: Grow Or Buy?

Chapter 5: Managing IT Talent In The 21st Century: Grow Or Buy?

Hopefully we can agree that the way that IT talent is being managed in most companies is just flat out broken. It's easy to point fingers and say that a process doesn't work; it's much harder to suggest a solution to the problem. Let's spend some time doing just that – the hard stuff.

Fix Suggestion #1:
Make and Buy Talent In Order To Manage Risk

Back in the good 'ol days of the 1950's and 1960's there really was only one source for new talent within a firm – you had to grow it yourself. This growing process took a great deal of time so extensive management development systems were created to track how the next "crop" of talent was coming along.

When an opening occurred in the organization, then either a new manager had to be harvested or else that part of the company and its associated opportunities had to be discarded.

As you can well imagine, the folks in charge of growing new talent would "plant" more talent early on in the process so that they would never be caught without someone to harvest should the need occur. Back in the day, firms could afford to have more talent than they needed. That doesn't work today.

If you are ready to be an IT leader and the opportunity does not show up quickly, then you are more than likely to walk out the door. Just to make things even worse, the Watson Wyatt consulting firm has done a study that shows that talent that gets trained and then is not presented with an opportunity to use that training will often leave the firm.

So what's an IT manager to do? Look, it will always make sense to grow your next wave of leaders internally as long as it is cheaper and less disruptive than going outside to get it.

However, there is no way that we can grow all of the talent that we'll possibly need internally. Since hiring from the outside is a much quicker solution as well as allowing you to be more responsive to dynamic business conditions, you really need to be able to use both solutions.

How to go about doing this? The first step is the simplest, stop trying to forecast your IT talent demand with any level of accuracy. Just admit it – you really have no clear idea how many people you are going to need 1, 2, 3 or more years out.

This wasted forecasting can be replaced with a different approach: simulations. Simulations won't provide a 100% accurate forecast; however, it can get closer.

What's even better is that if a simulation shows that the company's current plan will result in an enormous need for new talent, then the plan can be changed.

Here in the 21st Century the ease with which employees can leave a company means that developing too much internal talent is a much greater risk (and expense) than developing too little. Since you can go outside and hire the talent that you need when your needs exceed your home grown crop, there are four tradeoffs that you have to evaluate when filling a position:

- How long will you need this person? The longer that the person will be needed, the more likely you should be to develop internal talent to fill the position.

- How sure are you that you really know how long you will need the talent? If you are unsure of upper management's commitment to the company's current direction, then you should be less willing to develop internal talent to fill the position.

- Are Other IT Managers Available To Step In If Needed?: How specialized is the position – are special skills needed to perform the tasks associated with it? Could other IT managers easily step in to fill the position if required or would special training be required?

Now that we've come up with a strategy for HOW to fill positions using both internal and external talent sources, the next issue for you to solve will be to come up with a way to adapt to the uncertainty that every company has in trying to figure out how much staffing is going to be needed in the future...

Chapter 6

Staffing Flexibility Is Soooo Underrated!

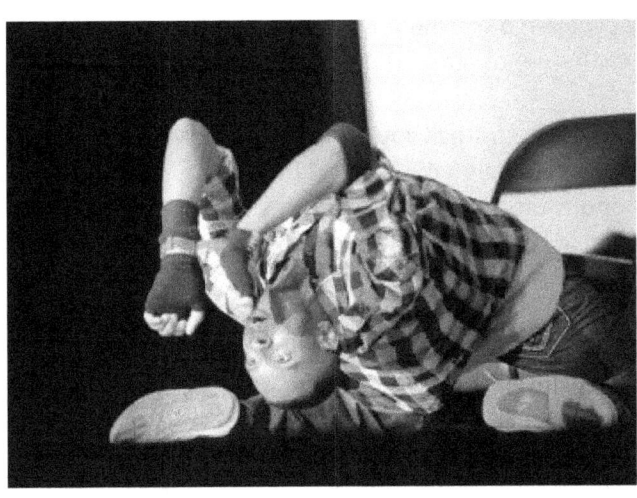

Chapter 6: Staffing Flexibility Is Soooo Underrated!

If you thought that it was tough to use your skills to manage your IT staffing needs using both home grown talent as well as warm bodies that you purchased off the street, just imagine how challenging it is when you try to move things up one level and adapt your IT team to the uncertainty in demand for IT talent.

Just think about that for a moment. How would your life be different if instead of running around trying to fill holes in your organization as they occur, you could actually be ahead of the 8-ball and be ready for changes as they came?

Here's a fundamental thought that will help you to solve this staffing problem once and for all. It's based on lessons that our supply chain friends learned the hard way a long time ago.

Instead of trying to stock your IT department with everybody that you think that you might need both today and for the next x number of years, instead do what the supply chain guys do. Bring in small batches of what you need more often. This will allow you to not have to attempt to predict your staffing needs so very far out.

For a good example of how the current IT hiring/staffing process is broken, take a look at how recent college graduates are brought into the organization. Most firms do almost all of their new graduate hiring right after the students get out of college.

This means there is a wave of new recruits that enter the firm in June. Even if you allow for some new-hire orientation and perhaps some training, the firm still has a need to carve out a substantial number of new-hire spots all at once. If the company is struggling in the current quarter, then this can be especially difficult.

A different way to handle this issue would be to take this single large problem and divide it into two smaller parts. Not all college graduates really want to go to work immediately after finishing 4, 5, or 6 years of intense schooling. Some would more than willing to delay their start date by 3-6 months.

If this was done, then the firm would only have to process half as many new recruits at a time. More personal attention could be paid to each incoming employee and better fits for talents and interests could be made.

Having fewer number of new hires to place but having them more often makes the staffing challenge much easier – you never have too many or too few. Retaining non-working students for 3-6 months can be as simple as agreeing to pay them 1/2 salary until they start working full time.

Long and expensive training programs present the same challenge. A two year management training program could be broken up into four 6 month programs. Each smaller program could have its own goals and forecasts. The benefit of doing training this way is that should an employee in training decide to leave the firm, then the entire training program expense may not have been spent on them.

Finally, within IT organizations different programs are often allowed to maintain and run their own talent management programs. The end result of this is that all too often, one program will have too many potential managers and another will have too few.

Since there is no centralized way to communicate these supply issues, the firm generally just deals badly with the imbalance. If talent management within the IT department was centralized, then this issue would not occur.

Chapter 7

What Should An IT Manager Look For When Hiring Employees?

NOW HIRING

Chapter 7: What Should An IT Manager Look For When Hiring Employees?

Talk about confusing! IT managers are responsible for bringing the best and brightest into your organization. However, in the field of IT, just exactly what this means is difficult to pin down – we keep changing our minds!

IT departments today look nothing like the IT departments of the 80's, 90's, and even early 2000. Once upon a time the best IT workers were those with the sharpest tech skills.

Then they were told to become more like the business side of the business. Next IT certifications were all the rage (I blame Cisco for this), next they were told to get really good at one technology, oh, but don't allow yourself to be pigeon-holed into just one technology. What's a nerd to do?

In a recent set of interviews with CIOs that Deb Perelman over at eWeek did, she discovered that they weren't really looking for specific skills such as SAP, Oracle Financials, or certain business skills when they did IT hiring. Rather they were looking for more of that touchy-feely stuff: enthusiasm, the ability to be flexible, and of course the ability to get things done.

What makes an IT worker different from workers in other departments at a company is that they need to be passionate about technology. Since technology is such a large part of the IT world, if an employee doesn't love it and want to be constantly finding out more about what can be done with it, then there is a good chance that burnout will occur sooner rather than later.

A love of technology does not mean that CIOs are looking for the classic "put 'em in the closet" techie. The ability to relate to others and share information is now recognized as being just as important as technology skills.

If CIOs ran the world (and they don't), then they'd be able to hire IT staffers who had lots of experience. What they are really looking for are folks who have done something over and over again so many times that it has become second nature to them.

What would make such a person an even better find would be if they had good industry experience in the industries that a particular company works. A key marker of this type of IT employee is that they often move in and out of the IT department to other departments such as marketing.

We all know that IT departments at most companies have taken a number of hits over the past several years. Downsizing, offshoring, and other events have taken a toll on IT worker morale.

CIOs realize this; however, they want / need their IT departments to be full of enthusiastic workers. It's important to note here that this is not a discussion about having a more youthful department – young folks can be just as glum as older ones. Rather, CIOs want elements of flexibility and excitement to come back into their departments.

What about all those certifications that were supposed to be our ticket to lifetime employment? It turns out that CIOs don't think that much of them these days. Instead, what they are looking for is experience and a history of executing projects successfully. These days it's really all about your ability to get the job done.

CIOs realize that the job market for IT professionals will keep growing. Things are going to get tricky because the Baby Boomers are getting ready to leave the market and the Gen X/Y folks don't have the numbers needed to make up for the exodus. What this means for CIOs is that they are going to have to start growing their own talent internally. All of a sudden that enthusiasm stuff starts to become a lot more important.

Chapter 8

5 Characteristics Of Hard Core Gamers That IT Managers Need

Chapter 8: 5 Characteristics Of Hard Core Gamers That IT Managers Need

As yet another generation comes to work in the IT department; IT managers are being confronted with another management challenge. More and more of the new wave of workers are coming from the world of multi-player online games.

These games consist of large, complex, social systems that are constantly evolving. Games like World of Warcraft and Eve Online are able to capture and hold the attention of their players because they are always new.

Hold on – before you throw your hands up in the air and give up on dealing with yet another type of new employee, you need to realize that this "gamer disposition" is exactly what you should be looking for in your department's workforce.

John Seely Brown and Douglas Thomas have done research in this area and they have discovered that that this type of experienced game player can bring 5 types of character traits to your IT workplace. These traits will help them to not only thrive but to also succeed in today's modern workplace:

1. **Focus On The Bottom Line**: In the games that these online players are playing, each player is constantly being measured and assessed. Each player is ranked and compared to other players using systems of rankings, points, and titles.

2. **Diversity Is Good**: Gamers realize that they can't do it all themselves. In order to be successful in a game, players need to build a strong team. The teams that are the most successful are the ones that consist of a strong

mix of both abilities and talents.

3. **Change Is Good**: Gamers thrive on change. The worlds in which they play are constantly changing – nothing is constant. Their actions transform the world in which they are playing. Gamers have come to expect this type of massive change.

4. **Learning Is Seen As Fun**: The games that players are participating in consist of complex challenges that have to be overcome. These challenges make the game fun. Discovering the tools that are needed and creating the knowledge that is needed to overcome challenges is what turns problem solving into a fun activity.

5. **Innovation Is A Lifestyle**: Gamers are willing to explore new ideas and ways of solving problems. Even when the solution to a problem is known, gamers are willing to search for new solutions that will solve the problem quicker or use fewer resources.

If you can learn to be supportive of the gamers who come to work as members of your team, then you'll have a workforce that is both flexible and willing to overcome stale ways of doing things.

Chapter 9

The IT Manager's Dilemma: Smart People Or Good Ideas?

Chapter 9: The IT Manager's Dilemma: Smart People Or Good Ideas?

When an IT manager is given an assignment to complete a project, who should he/she want to have on their team? Within the world of IT, there are many different types of people that you can choose from, but all too often it comes down choosing people who are as smart as (or less) that you or choosing people who are smarter than you are. What should an IT manager do?

Ed Catmull is one of the founders of Pixar and he is currently the president of Pixar and Disney Animation Studios (they merged just a while ago). He wrote an article for the Harvard Business Review in which he discussed how managers at Pixar deal with this problem.

Catmull is a firm believer that you really need to have the smartest people possible on your team – even if they are smarter than you are. In fact, Catmull is a firm believer that smart people are even more important than good ideas.

All of Pixar's films have been big commercial successes. However, there have been projects that have almost caused the company to fail. It's from these stories that Catmull has become convinced that having smart people on your team is a necessity.

Pixar's first big successful film was called **Toy Story**. After this hit, the creative team that made it got busy on Pixar's next film that was to be called **A Bug's Life**. Pixar also wanted to make a follow-up film to **Toy Story** which would be called **Toy Story 2**. Because the original creative team was busy, a second creative team was assembled to manage this project.

Originally Disney who was distributing Pixar's films at the time wanted **Toy Story 2** to be a direct-to-video release which meant that both the cost and the quality could be lower. However, Pixar decided that having two different standards for quality would be bad for the studio's morale and so Disney was convinced to make it a full theatrical release.

The way that you make an animated movie is to create storyboards which are crude pencil sketches of the movie's action and mate them with dialogue and temporary music. The result of this is called a story reel. As the team worked on **Toy Story 2**, these story reels were not improving like they should have been.

The reasons for this were many. The Directors and the Producers were not able to work together in order to meet the challenges that they were facing. One key point to realize is that there was nothing wrong with the story – everyone was very happy with the initial story. It's just that the team was having problems turning it into a compelling movie.

In the end, **Toy Story 2** was saved and went on to be a big commercial success for Pixar. How was this done? The original creative team was able to wrap up their work on **A Bug's Life** and they swooped in to save the day. The specific things that they did changed it from a ho-hum movie to an interesting one.

All Disney released movies have a happy ending; so this was never in doubt in the work that the original creative team had put together. The new creative team took this, tore it apart, and inserted several points in which a happy outcome was by no means guaranteed. This made the movie much more interesting.

Pixar's lessons from this project should resonate with IT leaders everywhere. Catmull says that the most important of these lessons *"...is that if you give a good idea to a mediocre team, then they will screw it up; if you give a mediocre idea to a great team, they will either fix it or throw it away and come up with something that works."*

The other lesson that IT Leaders need to learn from Pixar is that every IT department needs to have only one quality bar by which to measure each project. You need to be able to communicate to the entire department that it is unacceptable to have some OK projects as well as great projects. This is how you move beyond lip service for quality...

Chapter 10

Are IT Managers Afraid Of Commitment? Employees Speak Up

Chapter 10: Are IT Managers Afraid Of Commitment? Employees Speak Up

An IT department does not consist of just a bunch of servers and some cabling. It's really made up of bright, talented people who know a lot about how servers, networks, and applications can be used to propel a business forward. However, not every company and not every IT manager treats their staff the same way – do you think that that matters?

The real question here is how committed to their staff are companies and IT Leaders. Are the members of your team actual people or are they just resources that can be downsized or replaced at any time. In fact, does it really matter which way you choose to look at them?

The good folks over at CIO Insight did a survey of IT Executives awhile back and they uncovered some interesting discoveries.

Quite obviously, not all IT departments are created equal. It turns out that in the foreseeable future most of the hiring is going to be done by small and midsized companies. Given the current economic climate, that's good news. The other side of the coin is reflected by the larger IT shops which indicated that they will be reducing their IT staff (this includes IBM, Microsoft, and Yahoo).

Where things get interesting is when you take a closer look at who the firms that will be hiring are looking for. They want business analysts, systems integrators, networking staff, and web designers. These appear to be the place to be in IT!

But back to our original topic – what does it take for an IT Leader to get the people that he/she hires to stick around? The CIO Insight survey revealed that just paying more is not enough.

It turns out that what you have to do is to place organizational development up at the center of your IT recruiting and retention strategy.

In simple words, what this means is that in order to get your IT workers to stay, you've got to offer them things that they want like job security or work/life balance. Now an important point here is that when I say "job security", I don't mean offering a job for life (unless you are at Toyota).

Instead, what I'm talking about is having the company invest in the employee and having them develop skills that will serve them well in this job or in their next one.

In order to find out how to keep IT employees, you first have to understand why they leave. The IT Executives surveyed said that staff left for the following reasons:

- better pay / benefits
- opportunity to learn new skills
- reduced commute time
- to work at home or set own work hours

Knowing this, then what can an IT Leader do to get employees to stay? Focusing on improving every employee's work / life balance is a good place for a company and a leader to start. Keep in mind that the benefits that do the most to boost employee retention are the ones that provide long-term financial and career security.

Chapter 11

Why Are There So Few Women In IT?

Chapter 11: Why Are There So Few Women In IT?

The question that we're tacking here isn't if women are better than men at IT, but rather why are there so many more men in IT departments?

With no scientific backing what so ever, I think that a lot of us have made up our own reasons why staff meetings and all hands gatherings sure seem more like a frat party than a balanced gathering of equal numbers of both genders.

Some of the made up reasons for this include guessing that women have less interest in "hard" science that makes up parts of IT, women's educational experience makes them not want to go into IT, or that women are just not comfortable working in the male environment that is today's IT department.

As an IT Leader who wants to manage a balanced team of both men and women (the world is, after all, made up of roughly 50 / 50 of both), understanding why you don't have more women on your team is a critical issue that you need to resolve.

Vicki McKinney is an organizational consultant who, along with a number of academic researchers, conducted a study of 815 IT workers back in 2003. They published their results in the Communications of the ACM and what they uncovered was quite interesting.

The first set of questions that they asked tried to answer why a man or a woman would enter the IT field in the first place. It turns out that men were more likely than women to cite "love of technology / computers" as their motive. Women cited "job security", "ease of entry", and "flexible work hours" as their motivators for entering IT.

What this means to an IT Leader is that men are more driven by factors in an IT job itself. Women are more motivated by factors around the job. This is key knowledge when you are trying to motivate a team.

Another question that was asked dealt with role models. The ability to socialize is critical to advancing one's IT career and role models can help greatly with this.

The surprising answer that came back from the survey was that both men and women had a similar level of experience with role models. What this means is that women have had no problems finding men to act as their role models in IT.

You're going to like the next set of questions that were asked. This batch was designed to discover if there are any gender related differences in a variety of work-related experiences.

What's interesting is that the answer is YES. Specifically, women reported that their supervisors provided them with greater support in the meeting of their career goals and improving their job performance.

The final set of survey questions centered on career satisfaction. The result of asking these questions was that the researchers found no significant differences between men and women's level of satisfaction with their IT careers.

So what's an IT Leader to make of all of this information? Basically two things can be learned. Once in IT, women seem to be just as happy and driven as men.

They may have come to IT for different reasons, but once there they share many of the same experiences. However, IT has had and continues to have what the researchers call "an input problem": too few girls are being attracted to IT as a career path.

If IT Leaders want tomorrow's IT department to be gender balanced, then more work needs to be done to improve young girls' knowledge of computer careers as well as making them aware of computer related education. We all need to play a role in getting the message out...!

Chapter 12

Google's Staffing Problems Can Teach IT Leaders A Lot

Chapter 12: Google's Staffing Problems Can Teach IT Leaders A Lot

If you could go to work for any company out there right now, which one would it be? A lot of us would say Google – everything that we've read and heard about the company makes it seem like a great place to work. However, it turns out that even Google is not immune to IT staff problems...

Google's Staffing Problem

Google is in the middle of what is often called a "brain drain" – some of its best and brightest workers are leaving the firm to go join other companies. They've lost Tim Armstrong who was their advertising sales boss and they've lost David Rosenblatt who was in charge of their display advertising. Oh, and they are losing their top engineers to Twitter and Facebook...

What's Google Going To Do?

Google's plan to try to stem this exodus of talent is a typical Google solution – they're going to try and solve it by crunching numbers. Unlike many IT firms, Google has both the data and the processing power to attempt this.

Google plans on using data that they've collected from surveys and peer reviews in order to discover which of its employees feel underused. This may sound a little farfetched, but Edward Lawler who works at the University of Southern California says that eventually all companies will be approaching HR issues this way.

What's Gone Wrong At Google?

Using algorithms to find unsatisfied workers is clever and all that, but clearly there is something else going on here. Interviews with former Google employees reveal some interesting things about the day-to-day practical realities of working in this high-tech Shangri-La.

Former employees reveal that people are leaving because many employees don't feel that their efforts will make the same amount of impact as the company matures from its startup days. Compounding the problem is the fact that Google does not appear to provide much in the way of formal career planning. Often these tasks would be addressed by a company's Human Resources (HR) department, but it appears as though Google's HR department is viewed by many as being quite impersonal.

So What Should Google Be Doing?

As amazing as it may seem, the answer to Google's problems is actually very simple – hard to implement, but simple to describe. What they need to do is to put their customer first. By clearly communicating to the entire company that Google exists to serve their customers, a great deal of other staffing problems will fade away.

Final Thoughts

One of Google's biggest problems is that they have not found a way to keep their employees engaged. This isn't surprising because Google dominates its market and so it doesn't have any big competitors to use as a rallying cry.

Making its customers first would allow Google to focus its staff on a single goal that would extend throughout the company. All of a sudden every employee would have a way to measure the value of his/her work. Once again, this wouldn't necessarily be easy to do, but it's the right thing to do. If you can figure out how to do this with your team, then you will have found a way to transform yourself from an IT manager into a true leader.

It's from the forge of failure that the steel of success is formed.

Hard Work Does Not Guarantee Success, But Success Does Not Happen Without Hard Work.

- Dr. Jim Anderson

Create IT Departments That Are Productive And A Valuable Asset To The Rest Of The Company !

Dr. Jim Anderson is available to provide training and coaching on the topics that are the most important to people who have to manage IT departments: how can I build a productive IT department (and keep it together) while at the same time providing the rest of the company with the IT services that they need?

Dr. Anderson believes that in order to both learn and remember what he says, speakers need to laugh. Each one of his speeches is full of fun and humor so that what he says "sticks" with everyone.

Dr. Anderson's CIO SkillsTraining Includes:

1. How to identify and attract the right type of IT workers to your IT department.
2. How to build relationships with the company's senior management in order to get the support that you need?
3. How to stay on top of changing technology and security issues so that you never get surprised?

Dr. Jim Anderson works with over 100 customers per year. To invite Dr. Anderson to work with you, contact him at:

Phone: 813-418-6970 or
Email: jim@BlueElephantConsulting.com

Photo Credits:

Cover - By: SH Photography .de
http://www.flickr.com/photos/hegi_photo/

Chapter 1 - By: Nahuel Martinez
http://www.flickr.com/photos/meravoglia/

Chapter 2 - By: Amarand Agasi
http://www.flickr.com/photos/theamarand/

Chapter 3 - By: reynermedia
http://www.flickr.com/photos/89228431@N06/

Chapter 4 - By: James Kearney
http://www.flickr.com/photos/jaymzx/

Chapter 5 - By: Williamson
http://www.flickr.com/photos/4blueeyes/

Chapter 6 - By: U.S. Army
http://www.flickr.com/photos/familymwr/

Chapter 7 - By: Nathan Stephens
http://www.flickr.com/photos/groundswellzoo/

Chapter 8 - By: Sparky
http://www.flickr.com/photos/sparktography/

Chapter 9 - By: Ken Colwell
http://www.flickr.com/photos/kcolwell/

Chapter 10 - By: John
http://www.flickr.com/photos/mtsofan/

Chapter 11 - By: Department for Communities and Local Government
http://www.flickr.com/photos/communitiesuk/

Chapter 12 - By: Robert Scoble
http://www.flickr.com/photos/scobleizer/

Other Books By The Author

Product Management

- Product Development Lessons For Product Managers: How Product Managers Can Create Successful Products

- Customer Lessons For Product Managers: Techniques For Product Managers To Better Understand What Their Customers Really Want

- Product Failure Lessons For Product Managers: Examples Of Products That Have Failed For Product Managers To Learn From

- Communication Skills For Product Managers: The Communication Skills That Product Managers Need To Know How To Use In Order To Have A Successful Product

- How To Have A Successful Product Manager Career: The Things That You Need To Be Doing TODAY In Order To Have A Successful Product Manager Career

- Product Manager Product Success: How to keep your product on track and make it become a success

Public Speaking

- How To Give A Great Presentation: Presentation techniques that will transform a speech into a memorable event

- How To Rehearse In Order To Give The Perfect Speech: How to effectively rehearse your next speech to that your message be remembered forever!

- Secrets To Creating The Perfect Speech: How to create a speech that will make your message be remembered forever!

- Secrets To Organizing The Perfect Speech: How to organize the best speech of your life!

- Secrets To Planning The Perfect Speech: How to plan to give the best speech of your life

CIO Skills

- Critical CIO Management Skills: Decision Making Skills That Every CIO Needs To Have In Order To Be Able To Make The Right Choices

- How CIOs Can Make Innovation Happen: Tips And Techniques For CIOs To Use In Order To Make Innovation Happen In Their IT Department

- CIO Communication Skills Secrets: Tips And Techniques For CIOs To Use In Order To Become Better Communicators

- Managing Your CIO Career: Steps That CIOs Have To Take In Order To Have A Long And Successful Career

- CIO Business Skills: How CIOs can work effectively with the rest of the company!

IT Manager Skills

- Secrets Of Effective Leadership For IT Managers: Tips And Techniques That IT Managers Can Use In Order To Develop Leadership Skills

- IT Manager Career Secrets: Tips And Techniques That IT Managers Can Use In Order To Have A

Successful Career

- IT Manager Budgeting Skills: How IT Managers Can Request, Manage, Use, And Track Their Funding

Negotiating

- Learn How To Argue In Your Next Negotiation: How To Develop The Skill Of Effective Arguing In A Negotiation In Order To Get The Best Possible Outcome

- How To Open Your Next Negotiation: How To Start A Negotiation In Order To Get The Best Possible Outcome

- Preparing For Your Next Negotiation: What You Need To Do BEFORE A Negotiation Starts In Order To Get The Best Possible Deal

Miscellaneous

- Power Distribution Unit (PDU) Secrets: What Everyone Who Works In A Data Center Needs To Know!

- Making The Jump: How To Land Your Dream Job When You Get Out Of College!

"Tips And Techniques That IT Managers Can Use In Order To Correctly Staff Their Teams"

This book has been written with one goal in mind – to show you how an IT manager can attract and retain the right staff. It's not easy being an IT manager so we're going to show you what you need to be doing in order to hire, fire, and motivate the team that will make you successful!

Let's Make Your IT Career A Success!

What You'll Find Inside:

- "YOU'RE FIRED!" (HOW TO LET PEOPLE GO WITH CLASS)

- MANAGING IT TALENT IN THE 21ST CENTURY: GROW OR BUY?

- WHAT SHOULD AN IT MANAGER LOOK FOR WHEN HIRING EMPLOYEES?

- GOOGLE'S STAFFING PROBLEMS CAN TEACH IT LEADERS A LOT

Dr. Jim Anderson brings his 25 years of real-world experience to this book. He's been an IT manager at some of the world's largest firms. He's going to show you what you need to do (and not do!) in order to successfully manage your career!

www.ingramcontent.com/pod-product-compliance
Lightning Source LLC
Chambersburg PA
CBHW071813170526
45167CB00003B/1292